12 Good Traits Of A Leader

A Biblical Guide To Best Practices

~

Curtis J Alexander

Dedicated to my lovely wife Jenny, who has been my biggest supporter during the process of writing this book.

Table of Contents

Introduction

~

In this book, I will be delving into the world of leadership and exploring 12 traits that make a leader great. I will be drawing from the wisdom of Scripture as well as my own experiences and observations. I have been involved in church ministry leadership since 2001. I was in the retail industry for 29 years until I retired this year. I have experience leading paid teams of employees and also unpaid teams of volunteers.

In this introduction, I am listing in short form all the traits I think are key. This is not an exhaustive list but it should cover a majority of the aspects that make others want to follow you, whether you are leading a company, a department, a church, or even your family.

I am giving each of the traits their own chapter. In order to further develop our understanding of good leadership, I will also tackle each trait's "nemesis". A nemesis, in the movies or comics, is a recurring villain for a hero. These evil characteristics are the opposite (antithesis) to the heroic ones. Just like we root for the hero to overcome the villain in these stories, we also cheer on the leaders who seek to better themselves for the sake of their teams.

So every good leadership quality has an opposite negative trait, that can endanger a leader and his or her team if not properly identified and addressed. So here is the overview of the 12 "hero" (good) traits and their 12 "nemesis" (bad) counterparts.

<u>12 Good Traits of Leaders plus their 12 Nemesis Traits:</u>
1. Initiative- Recognizing the need, seeing what needs to be done and being the first to start on a path yet to be forged. (Nemesis: Passiveness)

2. Humility — Being teachable, willing to accept help when needed. Not bragging about yourself, but building up others instead. (Nemesis: Pride, the inability to accept help or correction)

3. Work Ethic — Willingness to roll up your sleeves and get to work. (Nemesis: Laziness, letting others do everything.)

4. Faithfulness — Your consistency, loyalty, and dependability toward the team and the project. It also shows you are committed to solid Biblical morals. (Nemesis: Unfaithfulness, Inconsistency, Disloyalty)

5. Discretion— This means we understand what is appropriate to say and what is not appropriate to say within a work environment. We respect others, their personal space, and their privacy. We discourage gossip. We keep sensitive information confidential. We communicate with tact. (Nemesis: Indiscretion. This nemesis is particularly bad because it can lead to harassment and inappropriate behaviours in the workplace).

6. Honesty — Leaders should be dedicated to the truth. We should be open and transparent

with no hidden malicious ulterior motives. (Nemesis: Dishonesty, corruption)

7. Vision and Planning — Seeing or imagining the path ahead and creating a plan to get the whole team there. Inspiring your team with the "why" that drives you. (Nemesis: Aimlessness)

8. Effective, Professional Communication — This is the ability to rally others to the cause, share information in a kind and efficient manner, and to listen to others with the intent to understand them. We as leaders should be approachable. (Nemesis: Miscommunication, which can lead to undue silence, confusion, harshness, and rudeness.)

9. Flexibility, Reasonableness— The ability to change aspects of the plan that aren't working,

accept feedback from the team, and try new things as needed. Leaders should be able to recognize when a team member has a better course of action than they do. (Nemesis: Stubbornness, Unreasonableness)

10. Knowledgeable — we need to do proper research and know the facts about our business and team. (Nemesis: ignorance)

11. Wisdom— This is the ability to apply knowledge. Wisdom is knowing what to do with what you know. (Nemesis: Foolishness, recklessness)

12. Respect and Trust— Building respect and trust with your team is key to success. (Nemesis: Disrespect, gas-lighting, narcissism.)

The traits are in no particular order. I cannot guarantee the responses of your team members. But following this advice will help you become a better leader.

Chapter 1 - Initiative Vs Passiveness

~

My wife and I were at the airport last year, waiting to board our flight to Nova Scotia. With time to kill, I started watching the planes taking off outside. I found the whole process fascinating. The planes have to undergo extensive checks, then wait in line, receive instruction from the control tower, taxi down the runway, in order to eventually take off. I am sure there are many details I am missing here, but the point is, the plane undergoes the initiation process. It starts. Without initiation, there is no take-off, no flight, no journey, and no arrival. I started with my airplane story because I find it to be a good illustration for this particular leadership trait.

Initiative is the first of the 12 Leadership Traits I would like to discuss. Seems fitting right? Initiative is what I took by writing this book.

Initiative is the ability to recognize a need, a deficiency, an opportunity, or an unfinished task, and without any external prompting, proceed to act on it. Initiative is also the ability to continue spotting issues and needs after the initial project has already begun. It's essentially the willingness and ability to start. Without initiative I would never have joined the writing platform called Medium.com in September of 2024. But I recognized my need to write and that this platform is a good place to do so.

King David took initiative when it came to preparing the materials needed for building a house for the Lord.

1 Chronicles 22:5 (New King James Version)
5 Now David said, "Solomon my son is young and inexperienced, and the house to be built for the Lord must be exceedingly magnificent, famous and glorious throughout all countries. I will now make preparation for it." So David made abundant preparations before his death.

It was David who took initiative to prepare all the supplies Solomon would need to build the house.

Zacchaeus took initiative when Jesus was passing by:

Luke 19:2-4 (New King James Version)

2 Now behold, there was a man named Zacchaeus who was a chief tax collector, and he was rich.

3 And he sought to see who Jesus was, but could not because of the crowd, for he was of short stature.

4 So he ran ahead and climbed up into a sycamore tree to see Him, for He was going to pass that way.

Jesus rewarded this initiative by calling for him, and visiting with him in his house.

A good leader has initiative in spades. You keep starting. Let's say you started your career. That's initiative. But then you continue to start, every single day, by getting out of bed and continuing that career. That is also an example of initiative. This trait takes courage because it may require you to start doing something different than other people. Or it may require you to "try again" at something you failed at before. Why? Maybe it's because you really feel passionate about it and are destined to succeed with it.

Initiative is not a one-time trait. It's like the "ignition key" that turns the engine on in a car. Now, I don't drive, but perhaps you do. Most drivers need their vehicle every day. So you need to keep starting your car every day if you want to go anywhere in it. The same is true with our careers, ministries, marriages, families, and lives. Initiative helps us keep on "beginning" again, each and every day.

Initiative can be as simple as telling your spouse "I love you" regularly, with no prompting. It can also mean doing the same job you did last week, because it needs to be done on a regular basis. Initiative is what separates leaders from followers. It's why some people can land management or leadership positions, as I did.

Here is an example: In my previous job as a grocery department manager for a store, I would recognize needs and act on them. For instance, most of our products would show up on ordering lists in the computer called "Assisted Replenishment Lists". When an item's inventory was low in the system, it would trigger the computer to add that item to the AR list. The person doing that order could scroll through the list and approve the system's suggestions and then send the order to the warehouse for shipping.

That order would then be delivered on the next truck in a couple of days. It's a good system, but a few of our items were not on any of the lists, and would get missed by the computer. One such item was a basic can opener. For a while, customers were asking for a simple can opener (we did sell canned food after all) and we never had any in stock. That did not make any sense to me. So I took the initiative to investigate this and discovered that no can opener was on the AR list. That's why our automated system was missing it. I did some digging in the system, found a product that was in stock in the distribution center, and ordered it through the hand-held scanner. We now had can openers in stock and proceeded to sell some every single week, at a good price and a good profit. I would keep an eye on our stock levels each week and reorder as needed. Initiative, among other things, is recognizing those kinds of problems and acting on them, turning them into opportunities.

<u>The Nemesis: Passiveness</u>

The arch-nemesis to initiative is passiveness. That attitude of "oh well, someone else will do it" is not a leadership mentality. This is why some people never become leaders. They are waiting for someone else to solve the issue. Now if it is not in our power to fix something, that's fine. Sometimes we must recognize that and simply trust God.

But what if it is in our power? Well, a leader will lead the way and act on that need. When you are given authority over a department or an office, you are responsible for guiding its success. When you work from home, that is your area of influence. What you choose *not* to control (tasks, problems, etc) is what you are passively *allowing* in your sphere.

So I figure there are three main reasons (and perhaps more) why people do not take initiative.

1. <u>They do not see or recognize the issue, the need, or the opportunity</u>. I think this one happens to all of us at one point or another. But for others, it happens all the time. When I was managing the grocery department at the store, I sometimes had to ask or remind certain employees to do certain tasks. Now some workers were excellent, taking initiative on their own. But others needed to be constantly prompted to complete an otherwise seemingly obvious task, one that they have completed before. If we always need someone else to tell

us what to do, we will never be seen as leadership material.

2. They do see the issue or opportunity, but don't care enough about it to act. Perhaps the employee does see the task, but they don't actually care. They wait as long as possible until someone finally tells them to do it. If someone sees a task they are paid to do, but does not do it until told, that's beyond passiveness — it becomes plain old laziness.

3. Other people in a different scenario may be too scared to act, if it is a complete change of life or career. Taking initiative sometimes means taking a calculated risk, and being courageous. So instead of forging ahead, they passively watch and let things pass them by.

I have had to fight off the arch-nemesis of passiveness in my own life. There were times I have seen a job, or task, and I knew it needed to be done, yet I kept putting it off in favour of other more pressing or interesting tasks. I think most of us have been there. None of us are perfect. We each can grow and learn in this trait.

To develop initiative, ask yourself questions like this:

1. Is there a hidden gem of an opportunity in this situation?
2. Is there any more I can do? How can I go the extra mile?
3. Is there a problem I can turn into a solution?
4. Have I taken the initiative to read all the information given to me?
5. Is it time for me to change what I am doing?
6. What do I have to offer that others need?

With proper initiative, preparation, facts, and planning, we can each "take off" into the skies of a new opportunity, just like that airplane.

Chapter 2 - Humility Vs Pride

~

When it comes to famous leaders, Moses may come to mind. Maybe it's because you watched Charlton Heston play him in the 1956 movie The Ten Commandments. Or maybe it's because you read about him in the Bible. Moses was said to be a humble leader.

Numbers 12:3 (New King James Version)
3 (Now the man Moses was very humble, more than all men who were on the face of the earth.)

Because of this he was able to take good advice from his father-in-law, Jethro.

Jethro saw how swamped Moses was trying to address all the issues of the Israelites by himself in the wilderness. So he told him something key:

Exodus 18:18 (New King James Version)
Both you and these people who are with you will surely wear yourselves out. For this thing is too much for you; you are not able to perform it by yourself.

Moses humbled himself and listened to his father-in-law's advice. If he was proud, he would have said "no no, I got this!". Then we would have had a very different story called "The Book of Burnout". Thankfully, Moses was humble and we got the story of Exodus chapter 18. He recognized his own limitations and took the advice to delegate tasks.

By reading the rest of Exodus 18 we learn that Moses trained up some more leaders under him who could handle much of the workload. Then, he would only have to deal with the most challenging problems. His team of leaders would handle the lesser issues for him. This is effective delegation — and every leader of a group (volunteer or paid) must learn it in order to make work sustainable. It starts by recognizing in humility that we cannot do everything, or at least we cannot do everything effectively when alone. And this recognition came from the ability to accept good advice. Every effective leader needs to be able to receive input from a caring and informed source.

Humility unlocks the ability to properly delegate tasks without being bossy. And humility also ensures that when a person starts to excel in the task you gave him or her, you will not get jealous or envious.

When you are humble, you know that it's not about you- the leader. It's about the team, the goal, and the success of everyone. When one of us succeeds, we all succeed.

Many of us leaders started off as workers, following someone else's lead. Then we grow through the ranks. I started in the 90's as a retail worker. By the early 2000s I was in a position of greater authority over a sub-department- the dairy and frozen food section. I was able to make merchandizing decisions, place orders, and give direction to certain staff members. This trend continued when I switched companies and was eventually promoted again to be a department manager. All this stemmed from my own work ethic to keep on giving my best and follow direction, and show initiative.

Now that I was a department supervisor/manager, I had to keep reminding myself that I don't have to do all the tasks myself. I can delegate. By keeping a humble attitude, I reminded myself that I cannot run the whole department alone, and that I needed those talented workers who were already in my section. I learned to delegate over the years, and to ensure I showed respect to the staff- and it was very empowering. Showing respect usually results in receiving respect back! I was then able to focus on my managerial tasks while the workers focused on the day-to-day aspects.

Mind you, I still worked alongside them and did the same work as them. When it comes to the industries like retail, this is a part of leading the team. (I will be discussing "work ethic" in my next chapter.) But I did not try to "do it all". I relied on my team, and celebrated their victories with them. When one team member wins, the whole team wins. Humility allows us to remember, and keep, that mindset.

The Nemesis: Pride

The arch-nemesis of humility is pride. An old proverb states:

Proverbs 16:18 (New King James Version)
"Pride goes before destruction,
And a haughty spirit before a fall."

Pride, or the haughty attitude, can be a destructive force against teams, people and businesses. I remember there were times I would receive correction from my manager for a poor performance or be shown a "better way" to do a task, and I always had a choice. There was a fork in the road. I could choose to resist the advice or professional feedback and dig my heels in... that's the "proud path". Or I could go down the path of humility, receive the feedback and improve. I have never been a rebel. But it used to be very easy for me to take things too personally and thus get offended. Then I realized that it's not about me, it's about the job. So as I got older and more mature, I became better at choosing the humility path, which allowed me to advance over time. Humility benefits everyone on the team!

Pride breaks relationships down, while humility builds relationships up. This is true in any category: work relations, friendships, marriages, and family relationships.

A proud leader is unable or unwilling to recognize the success of his or her team members or staff members. Instead of praising a job well done, they stubbornly pick on areas of improvement, and demand more from a team member. I think there could be an underlying fear or insecurity deep within the pits of pride. Maybe such a leader fears that another staff member will begin to outshine him or her. Maybe they feel their position is threatened by the excellence of others who are lower in the line of command.

Pride is often a mask we wear to hide our insecurities. But this mask is very self-focused, and near-sighted. It will damage any great team if the leader insists on wearing it. In fact, when proud leaders meet with success, they tend to hog all the credit, and barely recognize their team's efforts. And when faced with a failure, they almost always pass the blame on, rarely claiming any responsibility themselves. This is a sure way to damage company morale, lower productivity, lose sales, and maybe even lose team members.

Humility is when we take the mask off, and allow people to see us as real human beings, in a professional manner, with strengths and weaknesses. It takes more strength of character to be humble. As a side note, I should state that humility is not weakness. It does not mean we are a doormat. No, it means we hold the line, lead the way, and celebrate others.

Leadership is not about being perfect, it's about showing the way, admitting you need help (that's why you're a leader after all!) and gently guiding others. If it was a one-person job, you would not need to lead a team.

The best leaders are humble. They really care about the well-being and success of their volunteers or staff. They share the credit for victories, and take their share of blame for the failures. They can accept informed feedback, make adjustments, and build others up. They resist bullies, and manipulators, but refuse to play the same game. A humble leader is someone who stands their ground, and shows a better way, even when mistreated.

When you act humbly, like Moses did, and respect your team members, it will cause your team to rise to new heights.

Chapter 3 - Work Ethic Vs Laziness

~

Every day presents a choice. In order to make progress we must do those necessary, mundane tasks. Yes, even those ones we don't feel like doing. We do them today, and then do them again tomorrow. And then we do them the day after that. And it continues.

Good work ethic is consistently choosing to do these needed tasks with due diligence and a whole heart. If others see us working at it diligently, it will likely boost team morale. Leaders in the workplace (and in the volunteer world) should not point the way from the back row, but be ahead of the pack, showing the way. They lead from the front.

If you want your workers or volunteers to have a good attitude with good work habits, it starts with you. Industries like retail contain great illustrations of this. In my former position as a department manager for a retail store, I used to stock shelves just like the rest of the staff do, plus I would do my managerial tasks. I would work right alongside the team, rather than barking orders from the sideline. A leader is like the head husky in a team of sled-dogs. The lead husky pulls the team from the front. An ineffective leader will attempt to push the team from behind, and goad the workers. But effective leaders show their staff or team what good work ethic looks like, by demonstrating it. A good leader is the first to forge ahead.

Paul the Apostle told us:

1 Thessalonians 4:11 (New King James Version)

"that you also aspire to lead a quiet life, to mind your own business, and to work with your own hands, as we commanded you,"

So we are to "lead a quiet life" and mind our "own business" and work with our "own hands". Of course, minding our business can mean that we keep our nose out of affairs that do not concern us. But it also means we literally do our own business, our own job, and our own projects with excellence. We don't skimp on detail, effort, follow-through, or consistency. And we aren't concerned with who will recognize us. Instead we are concerned with the quality of work that we are putting out. We seek to do our best. We seek to be as efficient and effective as possible.

That kind of work ethic is a great example and can be inspiring to others.

Back to my former job as a department manager for a retail store. Certain employees did well when paired with a strong worker. But when paired with someone less experienced or less motivated then their own concentration and efficiency would suffer. Their work ethic depended on having stronger workers around them. So a leader (or a leader in the making) is one who works hard even when alone, and the boss isn't looking. They are self-motivated.

From doing household chores, to leading volunteers in a charitable organization, to directing an office full of employees, a good personal attitude and habit toward work is always beneficial. People are more inclined to follow a leader who "does" than one who merely "talks".

The Nemesis: Laziness, Apathy

Now to address the arch-nemesis to good work ethic: laziness. Some people hide behind the title of leader and use it as an excuse to pass off the work to others. This generally creates an atmosphere of dissatisfaction in an organization. People are likely to say "if my manager isn't doing anything, why should I?" Apathy in the workplace can spread rampantly if not addressed from the top down. I have heard from one friend who worked in a different company, and it was an apathetic workplace. My friend cared about his work, and demonstrated a good work ethic. But no one else would seem to care, not even the managers. It's baffling to me. I doubt any business or organization would last long with such poor work habits.

So it is crucial for us as leaders to be the example of a model worker. Now maybe your work is in a separate office and the workers can't see you working. Maybe they wrongly think you are slacking when you are actually working very hard. Well in my case, I would communicate to my staff what everyone including myself was doing because we worked in a store.

I would say something like "Person A, please fill the dairy section. Person B, please handle the produce department. I will handle the bakery section next." Then we would each proceed to accomplish our individual tasks. It worked quite well for us. Your situation may be different, but there is usually a way to communicate to your staff (without bragging) that you are working alongside them, as a "lead husky".

That's what makes a team. A leader gets into the front lines, and helps out. In my last chapter, I covered the leadership trait of humility. Well if we are humble leaders, we will remember our roots. For most of us, we had to work consistently, and efficiently for years under other leaders or managers. Eventually our work ethic was noticed, and we were promoted into leadership positions (such as pastors or managers). It would not make sense for us to abandon the trait that helped us arrive here in the first place.

Instead, let us each make that daily decision to buckle down and get to work. That will give our teams some inspiration.

Chapter 4 - Faithfulness Vs Unfaithfulness

~

It was an early, and dark September morning. Not very cold. I was a key holder, the first to arrive at the store, ready to open things up. I had been asked to arrive early, specifically at 6:45am exactly on all of my 7 to 4 shifts. So that's what I did. This particular morning was one of several when I was the first to arrive. But because the others were late, I still could not enter.

Despite me being on time, no one else was. It rendered my punctuality moot that day. That's because I was not supposed to unlock the store alone, for security reasons (which makes sense from a personal safety perspective). I followed the policy, and waited for back-up. This took another 5–7 minutes until another person showed up. I had arrived on time faithfully. It *appeared* to be for nothing because no one else was there.

Sometimes I would be there alone, waiting. Other times, people would be there with me on time and we could go in immediately. Whether or not others were punctual, I chose to keep going and be consistent. That's what faithful leadership is about.

I shared this story from one of my previous jobs, because I felt it illustrated the concept of faithfulness. Faithfulness, you might think, is just staying loyal to a company for 30+ years and never looking for other work. Well, you are partly right. That is one broad view of faithfulness. But it is becoming less common, less practical, and sometimes impossible, to stay at companies for long periods.

Sometimes, a company relocates out of your region, or goes under completely. My dad had to find other work when his company suddenly decided to move the office from Ontario all the way out west to Alberta. He was not willing or able to uproot his family. There was no guarantee that they would give him his job back anyway. So after 24 years, it was time for him to move on. He had been faithful, but the corporate world is full of instability and changing circumstances. This does not mean, however, that your attitude and behaviour should be unstable.

So I would suggest a more holistic definition for workplace faithfulness based on some ancient proven wisdom:

Psalm 5:9 (New King James Version) "For there is no faithfulness in their mouth; Their inward part is destruction; Their throat is an open tomb; They flatter with their tongue."

Luke 16:10 (New King James Version)
"He who is faithful in what is least is faithful also in much; and he who is unjust in what is least is unjust also in much."

Based on these two Bible verses, we can learn a little bit of what faithfulness is and what it is not. It is not flattery. It is not keeping a clean work station and timely schedule while secretly harbouring a plan for revenge. It is not unjust in its dealings. Faithfulness is just, and committed down to the smallest details. My company could count on me to show up and get the work done.

Faithfulness is stability and consistency of attitude and of conduct.

Faithfulness is an honest attitude of constant dedication applied to your job (and your whole lifestyle), regardless of how long or short your employment term is. You can be a faithful employee who works a job for 1 year, 5 years or 10 years. Perhaps you find something better and move on. But there is a faithful way to move on. And a faithful person shows stability in their performance for the whole term.

So, it is our attitude, our thinking, that dictates our actions. If you value a company, you'll respect their policies and procedures, even if you think some of them are less efficient. If you respect your fellow team mates, you'll show up for work on time. If you're sick, you respect the lines of communication and call in. Faithfulness is as much about following through on the little details as it is about the overall track record. It promotes company stability.

Proverbs 20:6 (New King James Version)
"Most men will proclaim each his own goodness,
But who can find a faithful man?"

Faithful people are a rare find these days. Whether it's finding a spouse, a friend, an employee, an employer, or a volunteer for your church or organization, faithfulness is a real gem. Employers are always looking for faithful workers. These are the workers they can count on, who don't give up easily, don't vanish from the office or workplace mysteriously, and remember to hand in their reports at the end of the day. They continue to work when they don't feel like it. This goes along with Work Ethic, the trait which I discussed in my last chapter.

A faithful person's mindset is obvious to others because their actions show a pure dedication which cannot be questioned. And when the time does come for them to depart from a company or organization, they do so with professionalism, stability, and courtesy.

I want to encourage you as leaders- your attention to detail matters, even if no one else seems to notice. Often, others do notice, but we simply don't realize it. Leading means we are the first to be faithful. We don't wait for others to start being consistent. A leader recognizes that their own example is what sparks the engine of consistency in others.

So your leadership of others depends on your attitude of consistent and honest dedication. Faithfulness builds a trust bridge between you and those who follow you. And as a leader, the best way to promote faithfulness to your team of employees or volunteers is to display it. Show them what stable work practices look like, and how rewarding the results are.

<u>The Nemesis: Unfaithfulness, Inconsistency, Instability</u>

And now to deal with this hero-trait's dark nemesis: the evil Dr. Late. Or he could be named Mr. Inconsistent. A good leader must be faithful — because it is very difficult to follow someone who is inconsistent, late, or sloppy on the details. In my starting story, people could only get into the building because I showed up first to unlock the door and let them in. If you don't show up, or make yourself available, then no one can really follow you.

Leaders who are always late, or are not stable in performance are less likely to have faithful teams. This does not mean all their workers are automatically bad necessarily. In fact, sometimes the workers show more stability than the management does. But in general, dedication and consistency starts at the top, and works its way into the rest of the team. A consistent and faithful leader is far more likely to attract faithful helpers and team mates.

Faithfulness sends a message. So does unfaithful behaviour.

A leader's faithfulness tells everyone "This organization is worth respecting! Let's work together every day and achieve our great vision".

Unstable, inconsistent habits clearly deliver the opposite message: "This organization is not that important, do whatever you want, whenever you want."

Now, does your faithful leadership mean your whole team will be stable like you? No, not always. Some workers just don't want to work, no matter what team they are in. Those people have a long hard road ahead of them as they will never get anywhere in life until they choose to be faithful. But that is their choice.

You can't make the choice for others. They must decide on their own that your organization, company, or church is worth respect and dedication. Your own actions of faithful stability will encourage positive decisions.

Please don't blame yourself if some volunteers or employees just vanish without a trace. Sadly, not everyone will respect your faithful and dedicated work ethic. I have seen it so many times. Some people just turn into "ghosts". And their choice to "ghost" an employer or a volunteer organization or a church is theirs alone. They are responsible for abandoning their own commitments. We are only responsible for our own attitudes and actions, not theirs.

Don't let it discourage you. Let us keep being consistent punctual leaders that show up on time, and handle the details each day. Let us be leaders who are determined to model faithfulness and stability.

Chapter 5 - Discretion Vs Indiscretion

~

Back in my days as a grocery department manager for a privately owned store, I had to use discretion on a daily basis. Here's an example.

One time, a person unrelated to any of our business dealings phoned the store and demanded to see our CCTV footage. I said, "No, we don't hand out private information to third parties. You can talk to the store owner on Monday."

The other day, my wife was asking a company online for a refund for a product. Most companies process these through secure portals or by mailing a check. But this company made a sketchy request: they asked her to send her bank info using unsecured email. My wife wisely refused to do that.

These are some examples of the many ways discretion can protect us, and our teams.

Other examples of discretion include not disclosing personal information to acquaintances or people you don't know that well. Maybe they visit your church, family or workplace semi-regularly. But that does not mean you owe them any explanations about your private life.

One time a young woman asked a married couple "are you going to have kids?" The couple's polite response was "That's a personal question." The young woman was well into her adulthood, but was clearly under-developed in her social skills. She did not accept that reply and asked again. The answer remained the same. The woman left "empty-handed", so to speak. Perhaps it would have been fuel for a rumour, or turned into a criticism. Her nosiness had been thwarted, but in a gentle and polite way.

When we exercise discretion, we help to establish proper boundaries. We know what is (and what isn't) our business. Leaders should be the first to show the way.

In general, people are quite uncomfortable discussing their private lives and plans with mere strangers or even casual acquaintances. The self-focused, indiscreet person does not understand this and presses for undeserved information. Such behaviour might be driven by insecurities, malice, immaturity, boredom, or rampant curiosity. No matter what the motive is, discretion is the bulwark against such prying.

You are well within your right to refuse to divulge any information that is not fit to be shared. I always recommend doing this with a gentle, professional, and polite approach if possible. When asked an inappropriate question at work, church, etc, you could respond in a manner like this: "I am not at liberty to discuss this. Let's talk about something else. Thank you for understanding."

Discretion in practice is a sign of respect. We refrain from asking people for personal, irrelevant or private information. Respectful leaders, pastors, owners and managers honour the privacy of those they lead and do not try to wedge themselves in where they do not belong. Discretion protects leaders from being indecent, or inappropriate. It helps a leader build trust with his or her team.

And discretion also guards leaders from revealing vital information to the wrong parties. This helps to protect businesses from things like loss, data breaches, and the theft of trade secrets. Discretion also helps to minimize employee rivalries. Perhaps one person has earned a bonus or a promotion. I am not saying the employer can eliminate all jealousy or rivalries this way... employees do talk to each other. But the leader's example can help promote a healthy environment where everyone works together peacefully, efficiently, and successfully.

You don't owe everyone in your life an explanation. Now, I do believe in being accountable to God. And we should be accountable within our own personal trusted network. Accountability is good. But meddling in the business of others is never good. Some people are just bored busybodies who should be working or doing something else that's useful. Instead they wander around, harboring a false sense of entitlement, wanting to know everyone else's affairs. They have no right to such information and will likely just turn it into rumor fodder or use it to pass undue judgments. This is a grave disrespect to people.

A discretionary leader will recognize this. As an assistant pastor, I am responsible for the spiritual care of our attendees and volunteers. They trust me because I respect their privacy when they choose to voluntarily confide in me about a struggle, concern, or question they have. I keep matters confidential.

<u>Ancient Wisdom</u>

There is some ancient Biblical wisdom we can learn from on this topic:

Proverbs 2:11 (New King James Version) "Discretion will preserve you; Understanding will keep you,"

And here is another quote:

Psalm 112:5 (New King James Version) "A good man deals graciously and lends; He will guide his affairs with discretion."

Everyone, especially leaders, should "guide" their affairs with discretion. That means we act with circumspect prudence and sometimes remain silent on a delicate issue. For those just starting out in the workforce, your prudence and wise attitude will gain you favour over time. Employers and leaders will begin to trust you and maybe even see you as "leadership material".

When deciding who to discuss things with, the "where" and the "when" is just as important as the "who". For instance, I may want to discuss an issue alone with my wife. So the time to do that is not in public.

Another example is from my time as a manager: I sometimes had to bring correction or discipline to an employee who had been acting out-of-order. I would never bring such corrections to them in front of the staff. It may be the correct person, but it would have been the wrong time and place. Instead, I always handled things discreetly and respected the employee by addressing the issue with them behind closed doors in my own private office.

Discretion will "preserve you". Among many other examples, it will protect your wallet, your bank account, your business profits, your balance sheet, your inventory, your marriage, your family, your employees, your employer, your identity, your ideas, your projects, and your church.

Discretion protects against many forms of sabotage. So we don't need to "spill the beans" to everyone who asks. And we can avoid discouragement by being picky about who to share our new ideas with. Some negative types can't wait to put down your ideas, or maybe steal them.

Discretion is very important in the world of money, too. We should be wise and prudent with our spending, saving, and credit card use, for example. This applies to both personal and organizational finances.

And discretion also ensures we don't "overload" our teams with too much information all at once. You may be sharing with the correct "people", in the correct "place" — but it may not be the correct "time" yet.

Jesus chose not to overwhelm his disciples with too much information all at once. He had already shared much with them. But then he used discretion to spare them from being overloaded with new details. Those details were important, but not at that precise moment. He knew to wait until they had time to process things.

John 16:12 (New King James Version)
"I still have many things to say to you, but you cannot bear them now."

So we, as effective leaders, will recognize the need to "space out" or time our communications with volunteers or staff. This will ensure they are not exhausted, frustrated, or overwhelmed with too much information or instruction all at once.

<u>Questions to ask ourselves</u>

Effective leadership considers the following kinds of questions before revealing any sensitive info:

"Who should I share this with? Who should not know?"

"When should I share it with them? When would be a good time?"

"Where should I communicate this information with them? What is the best location?"

"How should I share this? Is it more appropriate as a written correspondence, or as an email, or as a private verbal communication?"

"Why am I sharing it? Does this info further the productivity of the person I am sharing with? Does it help them in some way? Does it help the situation at all?"

"If I must share something difficult or sensitive, then how can I communicate it in a polite and professional manner, so as not to antagonize anyone?"

The above questions are examples of the kinds of considerations you should make before sharing anything with your team. It will help you in your workplace, your church, your family and your marriage.

Now flip it around and consider these questions if you are the "inquirer":

"Do I have a right to the information I am asking for?"

"Have I built a close level of respect and trust with this person?"

"Why am I asking? Am I legitimately involved in the family (or business)?"

" Do I need to know in order to do my job better?"

"Is asking this question being meddlesome? Am I giving in to boredom or curiosity? Is it to feed my rumor mill?"

Sometimes, it's best to just let something go, since it doesn't actually concern you. Other times, you'll absolutely need to inquire because you have a legitimate reason. Someone skilled in discretion will be able to tell these situations apart.

All discretion must be balanced with honesty, purity and transparency. Honesty is another good leadership trait that I cover in this book.

We must never use "discretion" as an excuse to hide illegal, immoral, or unethical behaviours or practices. Yet, discretion is always needed, as a positive "boundary line" to help guide us in our interactions with each other in every sphere of life and to prevent sensitive information from falling into the wrong hands.

<u>The Arch-Nemesis — Indiscretion, Oversharing, Harassment</u>

Now we need to tackle discretion's arch-rival, indiscretion. This negative trait plagues some homes, families, workplaces, churches, and also much of the internet. Some people simply do not know their place, asking way too many questions. These people often know they are being nosy and are prying on purpose. They manipulate or guilt-trip people into divulging information they have no right to know.

This goes for some leaders too. They share inappropriate sexual innuendos at work, or call people rude names. Tragically, some even go down the dark road of harassing or threatening their team members. That's unacceptable. Discretion in our actions and speech will prevent this.

This nemesis also rears its ugly head every time a spouse complains about their marriage partner in an open group. This harms a marriage terribly, especially when both spouses are known to the group. Indiscretion violates trust.

<u>Oversharing</u>

Some people have a naïve outlook on life. They trust way too easily. Thus they tend to volunteer way too much information about themselves to strangers or people they barely know. I know of one mid-aged woman who is sadly very indiscreet. She has been known to tell anyone what's in her bank account. Two other people were discussing their earnings in public within earshot of others. Now perhaps they trust each other. Fair enough. But it's not wise to share personal financial information so freely in public.

It's kind of like inviting anyone and everyone into your house. Don't be surprised when your jewelry pieces or electronics go missing!

Some unsavoury types will prey on such indiscreet behaviour. That's why I am emphasizing discretion: to encourage people to protect themselves.

We each need to say a lot less in public, as a general rule. It is for our own protection.

This is not to generate fear. It's to acknowledge the very real threat of predators, cut-throat competitors, and fakers who scam the innocent. Not everyone wants what is best for you, your family and your business. Maybe you are an inventor with a brilliant new design — you have plans to patent the design and begin production. It's vital you don't share your idea with the wrong person, who then might steal it.

So when in doubt, say less and listen more. Information about you and your family and business should only be shared with those who have proven to be trustworthy in your own sphere.

We as leaders should continue to hone our discretionary skills. These healthy boundaries protect us and those we lead. It ensures our whole team succeeds in the long run.

Chapter 6 - Honesty Vs Dishonesty

~

I recently found a 5 dollar bill on the floor at the church, before service began. It was not mine. I was pretty sure I knew who it belonged to as it was early and most people had not yet arrived. So I asked that individual and he said "Yes thank you, that was mine."

It feels good to be honest. Telling and living the truth is much easier than telling and living a lie. And as leaders, honesty is the only real long term plan for success. Understand that I am not denying the apparent success of some lying and dishonest leaders. We see them gain a foothold in business and politics. But that is a short-term gain, and a long-term loss. Truth always has a way of turning up later. It does not matter if that is one year later, or a decade later. The point is, truth has a way of surfacing on its own.

True leaders look both at the short term and the long term. They understand that in order for their word to carry any weight with others, it must be a true word. And honesty comes from a pure heart that wants to do the right thing.

See, if your team starts to detect lies in your speech, they will begin to take you less seriously. You will lose authority over time. I once worked for an assistant manager in a food and drug store years ago who consistently told lies. He drove a car that had a window held together with nothing but duct tape (I couldn't make this up!) His statements were equally as shoddy.

Here's an example I can remember: He once told me the new butter coming into the store is the "GayLea" brand (a popular brand here in Canada). And he said it with authority. Then when it arrived I stocked it and discovered on my own that he was wrong: it was some other brand. And he never bothered to correct himself. He just threw these statements out there, almost compulsively, with no regard for fact or reality. It was little examples like this that over time, caused the staff to respect and trust his word less and less. That is an example of ineffective leadership.

In my own time as a department manager, I would always admit when I was wrong. I always strove to give the correct and relevant facts to my team. In the rare instance where I had gotten a fact wrong, I would reach out and correct myself. This ensured the staff knew they could trust me. They knew I wasn't beyond reproach and that I always sought to be honest.

Now to balance that out I also used discretion. This means I only revealed the parts of the business that were relevant to the staff so they could be effective. I respected the privacy of the company by not revealing sensitive information to those not in management.

Honesty makes us feel weak sometimes. (I messed this up, or I don't know the answer, etc.)

I honestly don't have the answer for every problem. But in admitting that, you can now empower someone in your team to solve it for everyone. John C. Maxwell said in his book:

"A leader is great, not because of his or her power, but because of his or her ability to empower others." (*Developing The Leader Within You*, John C. Maxwell, Pg 9, Thomas Nelson Publishers, Copyright © 1993 By Injoy, Inc.)

If you are honest with yourself, you might realize that there could be people on your team who can do some things better than you. If you empower them, they will succeed, and so will you! Your whole team shines when you let individuals do what they do best within the context of your industry or organization. Productivity goes up, and the team glides forward effortlessly as a whole, complete unit.

There were times I wish I was more up front, admitting I made a mistake. I wasn't because I let fear get the best of me and I hid it. In the end, it would have been better for me to just admit my error, as the mistake was eventually discovered anyway. Adjustments were made, and business went on as usual. But it made me look dishonest in that instance.

I urge you not to make that mistake. Now all of us have made some kind of mistake and I am humble enough to admit that as well.

As time went on, I learned to be more open, not let the fear of being reprimanded take hold. So sometimes I would be asked for a sales figure or a price. Sometimes I knew off the top of my head and sometimes I did not. If I didn't then I would say so and go look it up. True I would still get reprimanded, rather unfairly (not everyone has an excel spreadsheet for a brain). But I had a good conscience. I would always strive to deliver the requested facts, figures, or results in an honest and timely way.

When I look back on those times, I wish the boss had been more reasonable. But that was out of my control. What was in my control was my own integrity and honesty. So I look back with gladness, knowing I was an honest manager, one who grew and learned from his past mistakes.

That is one of many reasons why I choose to be upfront with everything and not to let fear get the best of me. That brings me to my next point.

Honesty is a Sign of Strength

Honesty is not weak. It is only for the courageous and strong. Honesty shows your strength of character. You are showing your power when you are both discreet and honest at the same time. You are careful to respect privacy regulations, but you also do not withhold required information.

When we behave honestly, we protect the company and its profits. We ensure money does not go missing. We ensure inventory counts are accurate. We look after our staff, and make sure their rights are honoured. For instance, we ensure they get the required breaks and lunch periods. The list goes on.

Essentially, honesty and trustworthiness is what has allowed me the privilege of being a key-holder for three separate organizations over the years.

The Nemesis: Dishonesty, Corruption

Lying is a sign of weakness. And hiding the truth is a short-sighted goal. Eventually others will learn the truth, whether you are ready for it or not.

When promises are deliberately broken, what is behind it? Dishonesty.

When funds go missing or get embezzled, what causes that? The same.

In a store, we experienced dishonesty both from customers and from staff in the form of thefts or shoplifting. Dishonesty was the negative trait driving it. There was this idea that they could do whatever they wanted and not get caught. But it often did not go that way for them. I have been a witness to many shoplifters being banned from the store. Sometimes I did the banning myself. Sometimes the police had to be involved.

Repeated dishonesty eventually devolves into corruption. Such a terrible attitude degrades into greediness and pride and selfishness.

No one wants to follow a corrupt leader. This one negative trait is a real nemesis: among other things, it can bring leaders down, break companies, plague countries, and destroy families.

Being dishonest would have to be exhausting. The more lies someone tells, the more untrue stories they have to keep track of. Every time they need to reaffirm something, they run the risk of telling it differently. The longer they lie, the more people hear the lie. The more people who hear the lie, the more likely it is for the liar to "tell it wrong".

This tactic is used when interrogating suspects. When cross examining them, investigators will check to see if their story changes much when asked more than once. And if there are two suspects, the officials will separate them and ask for the story from each of them. If the stories don't line up, then that may indicate that a lie was told by one (or both) of them.

Living a false life is much harder than simply being authentic and living honestly. True, honesty comes with its own set of challenges, but those are the challenges of a hero. The life of a corrupt leader, on the other hand, is riddled with the problems caused by intentional deception, scams, and constantly trying to avoid being "discovered". There's no internal peace in that. Plus, upon discovery, the dishonest person often suffers grave consequences.

If convicted, they could end up under house arrest, in prison, or on community service. Plus relationships are in danger of breaking down in their life. And travel between countries becomes much harder (if not impossible) for those with a criminal record.

In the long run, honesty is what wins, even when faced with hardships as a result. Our inner conscience will be at ease. If we are honest, we can call out to God for help, for God only respects those who respect the truth!

John 14:6 (New King James Version)
"Jesus said to him, "I am the way, the truth, and the life. No one comes to the Father except through Me.""

Let's practice living in the truth. As honest leaders, we will ultimately gain more momentum, trust, and respect in our teams. It builds morale. Honesty is the effective way to long term success.

Chapter 7 - Vision Vs Aimlessness

~

Pop!

The bulb in the church's digital projector had just died in the middle of a live stream worship service. After that meeting, we would have to bring the projector in for a bulb replacement. That meant we would be without a way to show lyrics on screen for at least 3 more services over the next week. This was back in 2022.

As a pastor and worship leader, I am responsible for planning and leading our worship services at the church. And usually the digital projector is reliable. But every few years, the bulb gives out. This year I decided to be proactive and create -and order- several copies of a printed and coil-bound handbook of all of our most used songs, complete with a table of contents. That way, it won't affect our service too much if our projector goes out in the future. We can just use what I have nick-named the "Blue Book" (after its blue cover.) I had smaller booklets before this, but there weren't enough copies and only a handful of songs in them. The Blue Book was my definitive edition.

I use this as an example of vision and planning. Leaders are the ones who create vision for their teams. They can see far enough down the road to know what needs to happen, and then form a plan to prepare, and mobilize their team.

That popping projector bulb was the perfect opportunity for me to see down the road and plan accordingly. And to this day, the Blue Book works great- and some of our people actually prefer using that book now. It is the perfect safety net in case we lose that projector bulb again.

You may see an opportunity (or even a problem) in the distance. Now is the time to act. Leaders are the first to see the vision, create the plan, and then rally others to the cause. There is an old Proverb that still rings true.

Proverbs 29:18 (King James Version)
18 Where there is no vision, the people perish: but he that keepeth the law, happy is he.

Someone needs to guide the boat, see what's ahead, and chart the course. Otherwise the whole project or team might hit the rocks. A vision should be a written statement, or a visual chart, that defines what a company is about, what a team's goals are, and what the greater purpose or cause is.

When everyone on the team can see the written vision, it tends to make the smaller, more mediocre tasks more bearable. Every little task is then seen as contributing toward the purpose, the cause, the vision. That's because an effective leader tries to inspire his or her team with the "why". The best visions have a clear and motivating purpose.

Good leaders also make sure to put detailed day-to-day plans in place to align with the established vision. A vision is the long view or far off goal. Planning is the short term day-to-day process that gets us to our vision. That way, everyone knows their role and function and there is a minimal amount of confusion or misdirection.

Everyone can feel good and productive when they see the progress the whole team makes toward the vision, the goal, the purpose.

When I worked as a grocery department manager, I was responsible for flyer ad planning. I would look up what sales were on next week, and see how much of each item was on order, and map them out on a visual chart. I did this a lot with the frozen ads especially.

It was my idea to take the blueprints for the store, zero in on the grocery department, and take a photo. I then converted that photo into a black and white printout I could copy and reuse each week.

I found this effective because we used 38 smaller mobile freezers and the map clearly showed all of them. I would pencil in which items I wanted to go where. This was then pinned to the communication board in the stock room, so that my team could see my vision for next week's flyer ad.

Perhaps you have a vision too. Make sure your team knows what it is. Give them plans, and let them help you make the vision, the goal, into a reality.

<u>The nemesis: Aimlessness, Unpreparedness</u>
Now that we have established the need for vision and planning, let's explore what it looks like when those aspects are missing.

Nobody knows what the goal or end vision is. Everyone is uncoordinated. Morale is low because nobody knows why they're even working. "What's the point of doing this?", they may wonder. Time and money are wasted.

There are few things worse than a leader without a vision or a plan. It causes doubt in the team, and a general sense of unease. Leaders are those who look ahead and yet some leaders are not leading at all. They seem to be wondering and wandering instead. Lack of vision can only bring destruction and failure.

The leader without vision may be paralyzed by choice. There are so many directions we could possibly take our team: how can we know which choices are the best ones? A lack of vision will have us meandering down a path that could be a dead-end, or an endless loop. When we have a very specific vision, that will help us narrow down which choices to make. This may not necessarily eliminate all decision paralysis, but it should help you immensely.

The best way to combat a lack of vision is to refocus on what it is your company does and why they do it. How does your company help people? Who is your customer? What are their needs? What is it about your company that stands out from the rest? How can you capitalize on your team's strengths and make your group stand out? What are other companies in the industry missing? Why should the customer choose your company over the other competitors?

The way you answer these and other purposeful questions will help you shape a sharp, clear and inspiring vision. Then be sure to share that vision with the team, and adhere to it.

Or if you are leading a volunteer organization, or church, be sure you have clearly defined your mission statement. This includes what you do, and why you do it. That way, every decision you and your team make is a step toward that vision. A lack of vision and planning is what causes groups to waste resources and time. And a lack of vision will likely make a leader unprepared for problems that arise.

Vision is also the trait that gives leaders the ability to spot potential threats or challenges in the distance, and change course as needed.

Thus vision promotes our preparedness. After all, there are always obstacles in the way of any vision worth doing. We need to prepare in advance, with a plan to overcome each obstacle that lies between you and your vision.

Without seeing that worthwhile vision in the distance, we might be tempted to stare at only the obstacle and say "why bother?"

Vision is what gives people hope. It answers the question "why are we doing this?" It brings motivation to teams and it unlocks the potential to reach unrealized goals.

Chapter 8 - Communication Vs Miscommunication

~

When I retired from my previous job of 18 years, I was sure to communicate with those who would be taking over. There were certain aspects that they were not aware of, and recent changes that I knew about that were not clear to them. One young man in particular was so appreciative of my training that he gave me a thank-you card on my last day of work.

That's the power of communication. If you, as a leader, take the time to communicate to your team, they will more likely reciprocate and communicate with you. The thank-you card is one example of such reciprocal communication.

Each Tuesday evening, I hold a practice session for the volunteer worship team at our church. In it we discuss any new songs, or previous ones we need to brush up on. Most importantly, I share my plans for the next few services with them. That way they know what songs I plan to do in the Thursday and Sunday services.

Communication, then, is a sharing of information, ideas or thoughts. It can be verbal, or non-verbal (using gestures). It can be written, or visual (using photos or symbols). Even a street sign with a triangular "yield" symbol is communication.

Information is valuable. Knowledge is precious. Wisdom is key.

But...

If you don't share it, then the value stops with you, and things could break down. Communication is really the sharing of your wealth of information and strategies and insights.

Now we already covered the good trait of discretion in a previous chapter so I won't belabour the point here. But discretion is knowing *what* to communicate, with *who*, and *when*. It also means knowing what *not* to communicate. But discretion is pointless if there is no communication at all.

<u>Communication is Fundamental to Team Success</u>

Communication is fundamental to any successful business, church, or volunteer organization. It is like an organization's life-blood.

1 John 1:4 (New King James Version)
4 And these things we write to you that your joy may be full.

The Apostle John, in the above verse, notes the reason why he was writing to the church. Writing is a form of communication. And John's communication was in order to enrich that church's joy.

From morning greetings, to good-byes at the end of a work day, effective and professional communication is absolutely vital to establishing a warm and friendly work environment. Saying "please" and "thank you" are also basic and important building blocks of communication. The way in which we communicate is just as important as the information which is contained within that communication. Rudeness only undermines communication. Rudeness can show up in speech, tone of voice, actions, or gestures. We must always strive to be polite on purpose. Be intentional about it.

Clarity is also key. Many times, I would ask for a task to be done, only to find that it was only partially completed. That was sometimes because I failed to give enough information or was not clear enough on what I wanted. So it can happen to any of us. Rather than get upset at the worker for leaving the task incomplete, I would first review in my mind if I had given that person a clear enough set of instructions. Not every manager understands this.

Communication is a 2-way street. It is my responsibility to clearly convey with professionalism what I want the worker to do. Then it is the worker's responsibility to ask for clarity where needed. If both parties understand this, it can accelerate productivity and success.

For this reason I often found that leaving my team a concise list of tasks on paper was a great way to communicate what I wanted accomplished. In your organization, it might be an encouraging and inspiring email sent out to the whole team which details the strategies and goals for the next week.

The Nemesis Trait: Assumption, Miscommunication

Working in a grocery and fashion department store, we would often get questions from customers. Some of these fine folks did not understand the importance of being specific in their requests.

One time, a customer asked me for "muffin mix". I took him right to the shelf where it was. His impatient reply was "this isn't muffin mix!". I said "yes sir, it says so right on the bag here."

Realizing we had reached an impasse, he finally came out with words (real words!) that revealed what he was actually looking for. These were necessary words that he had failed to speak at the beginning. He finally muttered, "It's not oatmeal muffin mix".

I replied, "I see sir, well you did not ask for oatmeal specifically. Sorry but we don't have that kind."

Then he was silent, probably realizing he had failed to communicate enough information about what he wanted. I could have saved him 5 minutes and a lot of pointless dialogue if he had been more specific in his communication from the start.

That's right, mind-reading is for science fiction only! In the real world, we must use some form of outward language (spoken word, written text, sign language etc) to effectively communicate what is on our mind.

This extends to everyone. Whether you are a customer, a client, a volunteer, a pastor, an employee, an employer, or a self-employed person, you should always value the power of clear and concise communications. Never assume the other party "already knows" what you do.

But, unfortunately, the tendency to assume is strong in human nature. If someone is silent, we assume they must be mad, or perhaps that they don't care. If someone gives us a request, we assume there are no more details to it. If the leader doesn't speak (or otherwise communicate) about a potential problem, the team may assume that all is well. And if a leader doesn't tell his or her staff when they are doing well, that team may assume that things are going poorly.

It is so natural for us to assume. In the absence of dialogue, our minds actively seek to fill in the details. And that is how confusion or wrong ideas begin.

And sometimes we do communicate, but leave important parts out. We forget to bring those details out of our minds, and into the known universe where others can hear or read them.

We forget that people really cannot read our minds. Leaders and teams alike can forget that a partial description is not a complete one.

I may be feeling very strongly about something and I could assume that others know how I feel. But no. It is *not* obvious what I am thinking or feeling.

We must remain vigilant when it comes to communication. I should not assume that others know what I mean.

I have encountered leaders who, after giving vague instructions, get upset when workers ask for details. Why? Because that leader does not understand the basics of communication.

Patience is required in order to account for all the different ways in which people listen and learn. And as annoying as it sounds, we must sometimes repeat ourselves. Even clear instructions can be misunderstood or misheard. A wise leader will understand this and patiently repeat instructions or information as needed.

The way a leader gives an instruction and the way the team member understands it could be two different things.

In the book *Lead Like Jesus* By Ken Blanchard, Phil Hodges, and Phyllis Hendry, they point out the need for managers to test for understanding. Before sending the worker to do the task, we should ensure they repeat the instructions back to us. If the team member is able to repeat things exactly, it's a good indicator they understand the assignment. Otherwise we may end up with an entirely different result than the one we wanted.

For instance, I could ask a worker to "please move those tins of coffee from the back end cap to the front end cap."

That sounds clear right? Well, not necessarily. What if there are two possible front end caps? I must not assume that the employee will instinctively know what one I am referring to. That will only lead to a waste of time and effort. This is an example of miscommunication. Sadly, it happens too often, in many different organizations. But it can indeed be avoided with a little extra effort.

<u>The Sound of Silence</u>

Another bad aspect of this nemesis called miscommunication is unwarranted silence.

I have known situations in a company where something major occurred. But the leader did not communicate anything to those it affected- at least, not right away. The staff and supervisors were left to "deduce" things on their own. There was no guidance or effort to bring stability through discreet dialogue. The work environment was a bit unstable.

Silence can make a leader seem distant, and that you really don't matter to him or her. Assumptions could run rampant. And then, the rumours arise. In the absence of good information, the staff or team might generate their own "versions" of events and that then becomes a falsehood that spreads in the workplace.

Silence can be a deadly form of miscommunication. It leads to misunderstandings, tension, unease, and poor performance.

How to overcome Assumption and Miscommunication

Leaders should be the first to communicate. And they should not assume their way of speaking or writing can only be understood one way.

Taking leadership of communication often means asking more questions. If you are not sure that your information or instruction was understood, you can take the lead by thoughtfully asking things like:

"Did you understand the task?"

"Would you like more details?"

"Could you repeat the task back to me in your own words?"

Or perhaps you are receiving info. Then you could politely ask:
"Could you give me more specific details please?"
Leaders will know when the right time to share is. Breaking the silence often puts staff at ease and helps them gain a realistic outlook. Breaking the silence can also destroy any rumours that may be floating about. I understand that a leader cannot necessarily divulge sensitive information to all parties. We covered that in the discretion chapter. But a good leader will continue to make an effort to reach out to each person in the team, and prevent the workplace from becoming an

empty vacuum. Good leaders keep communication lines open and safe.

Doing so will give the team:

-A sense that you care about them.
-The information they need.
-The instructions that will produce success.
Let's lead the way by practicing effective communication skills.

Chapter 9 - Flexibility Vs Stubbornness

~

The CN Tower, in Toronto, Ontario, stands at an impressive 553.33 meters (1,815 feet, 5 inches) tall. Its construction was completed in 1976, making it the tallest free-standing structure in the world at that time. The world has since seen the arrival of even taller structures. Yet the CN Tower is still the tallest in Canada.

I wanted to talk about it because of the amazing engineering that went into it. One example of this amazing design is its ability to withstand the fierce winds that can gust off of Lake Ontario. This comes due to its flexibility in adverse situations. It can actually bend and flex in the wind a few degrees. To counteract this slight movement, there are weighted rings in the antenna and also steel cables running up and down the whole tower.

Proverbs 18:10 (New King James Version)
10 The name of the Lord is a strong tower;
The righteous run to it and are safe.

Like the CN Tower, a leader needs to be able to stand firm, yet stay flexible in certain situations. We need to be reasonable and stay open to adjustments when things are not working as they should.

For example, I am an assistant pastor and worship team leader. I will sometimes add new songs, or write new songs, to add to our list for services. While it is rare, there is the odd time my song pick does not work as well as I thought it would. After getting feedback from the other pastors and my team, I may drop a song after a few services. Or I may edit the lyrics after receiving some feedback (especially my own lyrics). I choose not to take things personally. Sometimes, it's best to "go with the flow" and release your "pet idea" back into the wild. Certainly, humility plays a huge role in being reasonable and flexible like this.

Leaders with too much pride cannot recognize that they are not always right. This does not necessarily mean they are failures. It's not a judgment against them personally. It simply means they need to flex with the situation. Flexibility, to a limited degree, is healthy. It allows the CN Tower to withstand high winds. And it helps us keep on standing as well. When a leader is flexible, it shows your team that you are reasonable, approachable, and easy to talk to.

Earlier this year, back when I was a store department manager, I would sometimes have to approve merchandise or grocery returns at the service desk. Most of the time, the customer would have the required receipt and there would be no issue. But sometimes, there was no receipt. The customer would lose it, or forget it at home. This is where flexibility would come in. Our store had a flexible return policy.

So if the customer did not have the receipt we could often still process the return for them if they had a valid photo ID. There were some exceptions and restrictions of course. But many times, I would be called to the front and the customer was looking to return or exchange a carton of half and half cream that had gone sour early. Most people do not save their receipts for such a purchase so I always approved that particular kind of return or exchange.

Of course, for more pricey items, there was always the option to refuse a refund without a receipt, especially if our store computer had no records of a purchase being made, or if the item was not listed at all in our database.

If I did grant a refund for something like clothing, it was often with encouragement to keep their receipt for future purchases (because our computers would only allow for 3 no-bill refunds total per customer). That's like those counter-weights in the CN Tower's antenna. It keeps a leader from being taken advantage of.

I often worked at night, and supervised during closing shifts at the store. On rare occasions, one of the employees would ask me for permission to make a last-minute purchase before the store closed. Generally, employee purchases were to be done during breaks and meal periods. I would usually approve the request even though their break was already done. But I would accompany that allowance with a reminder not to make a habit of doing last-minute purchases on the clock.

Now, there are situations where the manager or leader cannot deviate at all from a course of action. This might be because it is dictated to him or her from higher levels of authority. Or there might only be one effective way to get a certain kind of job done. Or it would threaten the safety of the workplace.

Flexibility is not the same as being a push-over. Far from it. If the tower swayed too much, it would fall over. But there are checks and balances in place to prevent that from happening. The same is true in the workplace.

For example: Health and safety policies are put in place for a reason. They are meant to protect the workers, customers and the company. Corners should never be cut when it comes to these rules (Rules like the use of PPE -personal protective equipment, or proper training on heavy equipment, etc.).

While a little bit of flexibility is good in general, it's also important not to misuse it.

<u>The Nemesis: Stubbornness and Unreasonableness</u>

Proverbs 6:15 (New King James Version)
Therefore his calamity shall come suddenly; Suddenly he shall be broken without remedy.

There are stubborn leaders and managers out there who don't even listen to their staff or team members. They refuse to entertain new ideas from the team, some of which might be quite good. Other leaders stick to all the rules so tightly that they don't allow for special circumstances and emergencies.

An example of this is the store's food and drink policy. The store where I worked had signs prohibiting the consumption of food or beverage in the store. And we would enforce this policy. Customers had a tendency to spill their coffees and foods, thus creating slipping hazards on our sales floor and other health concerns. But there were times a customer with diabetes would have their blood sugar go low, and they needed to have a sweet drink immediately. In cases like that, we allowed it. This is an example of being flexible with certain rules.

Being too stubborn or brittle in our methods and attitudes may eventually lead to breakage. It could be a breakdown in the team, the leadership, or a failure in the company. Something could give out.

It's kind of like a big old tree that snaps in a wind storm and falls over. I've seen my share of broken tree trunks and branches in my area of Ontario over the years. There was a major wind storm in 1998. Trees were broken or toppled over, and tree branches were strewn all over the streets and parks. Some large trees were uprooted, and pushed into nearby buildings. One pine tree in our neighbourhood fell on a house.

Then there was the more recent wind storm in 2022. That year, a major wind storm blew through southern Ontario and several older trees were broken or blown over. In my mother's backyard, two large old willow tree trunks snapped in half and fell over. They no longer had the flexibility or give required to weather the storm. Thankfully, the broken trunks missed the back deck, so no serious damage was done to the house.

In every wind storm, there is quite the mess for crews to clean up.

This is an illustration of what can happen to us as leaders as we get too set in our ways. We are skilled and experienced. We've been using the same tried and true methods for years. But then circumstances change. New methods or ideas are sometimes needed. New efficiencies are found.

For instance, in the 90's I worked in a store where we wrote our store signage by hand using black and red markers. The product name and size was written in black, then the price was added below in red.

As I moved to a new company in the mid 2000s, I had to learn a computer program that allowed staff to print signs automatically. They looked a lot better and took way less time to produce.

Indeed the best leaders are able to stand strong and be dependable, faithful, and unwavering in their dedication. But they also recognize when the ship is liable to run aground. They can see when a practice is no longer working, and a new method is required. The first company I worked for no longer exists. The second company I mentioned above is still going strong as of the publishing date for this book.

In more recent years, staff would sometimes come to me with ideas for merchandising. I would not simply dismiss them. I would consider their idea, see if it lined up with the overall plan and vision of the store, then give a thoughtful reply. Sometimes I would go with their suggestion, other times, I would not. But they always knew I was listening to them. That's what makes a leader reasonable.

Other managers or leaders, however, have chosen a more unreasonable approach. New ideas would be shot down immediately and some kind of scolding would ensue. That is a great way to kill off new talent and squelch employee growth. If team members are chided for suggesting something new, that company will likely suffer some stagnation eventually. Team members are going to stop confiding in their leader and respect suffers.

Leaders should be like that tower. They can stand strong, yet are also able to sway, to a certain degree, when needed.

Chapter 10 - Knowledge Vs Ignorance

~

Have you ever written a grocery list, only to go to the store without it? I hate that "listless" feeling.

Leadership is the same way. We need to know the facts. We need to take inventory of the situation. Our team relies on us having the proper information.

Proverbs 15:14 (New King James Version)
The heart of him who has understanding seeks knowledge, But the mouth of fools feeds on foolishness.

Good decisions can only happen when we have all the necessary facts, numbers and related statistics.

Facts are, well, a fact of life.

A good leader takes the time to collect all the data he or she needs, and process it into meaningful formats or charts. It's only when we get all the data together that we can start to see a bigger picture regarding the direction a business or organization is going in.

How we "feel" about our team and progress may be something entirely different than what the facts say about it.

In my time as a grocery manager for a department store, we had some days that were very busy, and the sales figures proved it.

Other days, it felt very busy, but the sales numbers told a different story.

Another example from retail: I made sure to prepare for the upcoming truck load days. I would review the order using the computer, and have my list ready. I would know what items were going on sale next week, and how much of each of them would be coming in this week. I could then make plans with that information, and communicate to the staff where each item should be merchandised.

How Much Pasta?
In retail, you need to know how much of an item you have before you can make a merchandising decision. And guessing at it is bad, because that runs the risk of a "redo". Redos cost time and money and extra labour.

If I had 1,080 single units of bagged pasta (45 cases), for instance, it would not make sense to merchandise it on a short end. There's not nearly enough holding power there. We would plan for 2 full (tall) ends and also a large display on a pallet on the sales floor.

Most of the time, our warehouse skids came mixed. This means it would be difficult to "eyeball" the quantities visually. Going back to our dry pasta example, our warehouse would usually put items like the pasta on three or four different skids. It looked like a smaller quantity because of how scattered everything was.

But looks can be deceiving. This is why printing out the actual quantities in advance is valuable. Knowledge is what stops you from "winging it." Often the staff would ask me for the quantity of an item or how many varieties there were within a particular ad grouping. I was able to give them the answer, because I had come prepared with my numbers.

<u>Booooring!</u>

Now I know that facts and numbers can be boring to some people. And if you are anything like me, then numbers don't always "stick" the best in your brain. This is especially true when so many figures are being thrown your way, and things are always changing.

That is why I used printouts and written lists. These lists were an extremely helpful tool to me, that boosted our productivity as a team, and eliminated guess work. I made a habit of keeping the relevant information on hand, to help our staff as needed.

<u>More Than Just Numbers</u>

Knowledge is not just a numbers game. As important as stats and sales figures are, there is so much more to it. You also need to know your people. Some leaders are strong in their knowledge of numbers and statistics, but weak in their knowledge of people.

Gaining the proper knowledge of a situation extends to getting feedback from staff and/or customers. It really applies to any situation involving people. As writers, for instance, it really helps us to write better, if we understand our readers.

If we get a genuine understanding of the thoughts and attitudes of those we serve and lead, it will help us adapt our approach accordingly.

For instance, if one staff member came to me with a concern, I would now have new knowledge. I could then discreetly do an investigation to verify things as needed. Then I would act in a professional and timely way to address and resolve the concern.

The reality is, if you don't listen to your team, and observe them, you are missing vital information. Knowing your team is as important as knowing your product, your sales figures, or your sermon outline!

The Nemesis: Ignorance

One of the worst villains of all time is the trait called "ignorance". Some leaders think they know it all, but are actually quite ignorant in some aspects. Other leaders may realize that they lack info, but don't bother to do the needed research. You may have heard the saying "ignorance is bliss". Well, I would tend to disagree, especially for the long-term health of a team. Ignorance makes for a poor leader.

Sure, one might barely survive for the short term in ignorance. But that will not last for long. Jesus shows us the value of knowledge with the following parable:

Luke 14:28–30 (New King James Version)
28 For which of you, intending to build a tower, does not sit down first and count the cost, whether he has enough to finish it —
29 lest, after he has laid the foundation, and is not able to finish, all who see it begin to mock him,
30 saying, 'This man began to build and was not able to finish'?

Here in this parable, Jesus is telling his listeners that ignorance is *anything* but bliss. In the case of the lead architect, ignorance might cause him to start the building project, only to run short on money or supplies half-way through. Then everything spent up until that point would be wasted.

In the world of leadership, ignorance can only lead to loss. Loss of time, loss of resources, loss of money, loss of productivity, loss of opportunities and even a loss of team support.

We have seen from the Biblical example given above that ignorance toward numbers and money is bad. But ignorance toward people can be even worse. A leader's greatest asset is his or her people- the team.

Ignorance toward people is quite awful. A leader with an ignorant attitude may lose some very good people over time. A team leader or manager may be brilliant with the stats and the finances. They may have all the ordering down to an art, and have all the inventory in check. But poor treatment of staff or volunteers will still lead to loss over the long term. Some leaders do not make the effort to connect with their team members, and to understand them in vital ways. This only leads to a disconnected, and out of touch, form of leadership.

Let's go back to the story of the hapless tower builder for a moment. Let's just say he did have the money and the materials. But he still failed to complete his tower. Why? Well, perhaps he did not pick the right workers for the job. Or perhaps he hired good employees, but treated them poorly, and rudely. As a result, they left.

Overcoming Ignorance Is a Choice

So we must each choose to know. Knowledge is within reach for those who want it. Ignorance does not have to be a problem. It starts with acknowledging that we do not always have the information required- yet. Only God knows everything. A good leader recognizes that they do not always have the facts. It is unhelpful to be a "know-it-all". The "know-it-all" rarely knows much.

It is also unwise to flat-out ignore the unknowns, especially when it comes to facts that are readily available to us. It's not enough to shrug our shoulders and say "I dunno."

Once we acknowledge that we need more info, we can choose to find it. Here are some examples:

Take a moment and pull up those sales figures.

Research the order quantities you will need to stock your shelves.

What is the click-through ratio for your latest ad? What percentage converted to sales?

What products are people in need of these days?

Are the bills getting paid?

This takes determination and a conscious effort. And the time taken to do research like this will actually save you more time down the road.

Also we must show a keen interest in our teams. People are what make a team possible. Gain an understanding of your team. Seek knowledge like the following:

What is the general attitude of the team?

Are the team members feeling respected by you?

Does each team member have the resources needed to complete their tasks?

Is anyone feeling overworked, or stressed?

Are tasks being properly delegated?

Is there a healthy sense of optimism or are people generally negative?

What are the dynamics between team members? Is each person meshing well? Is there any area of conflict?

These are just a few examples of the kinds of facts you should know about your team. Of course, every situation is unique, and you may need to ask different questions than the ones shown above.

When the team sees the leader making an effort to get feedback, it will boost morale. You can have both the "stats" and the "people facts".

And that will effectively inform your leadership decisions.

Chapter 11 - Wisdom Vs Foolishness

~

I watched a series of high-rises going up in my neighbourhood over the past 7 years and saw them at their various stages. The builders always start by digging down first, and establishing the foundation. That takes a lot of resources and effort, but is crucial to the stability of everything that will be built on top. That's wisdom.

Sometimes we have plenty of facts, and know all the pertinent details. But we still don't know what to do. This is where wisdom comes into play. As important as knowledge is, it still needs to be applied correctly. Wisdom is applied knowledge. Sometimes we are faced with multiple choices and options, because of all the facts presented to us. That can be confusing. Wisdom helps us start off, and continue, correctly.

That's why we need wisdom as leaders. It helps us apply or use our knowledge in correct and successful ways. When we act in wisdom, we will meet with success.

The Bible puts it plainly:
"...Wisdom brings success." (Ecclesiastes 10:10b NKJV)

Metaphorically, knowledge could be considered the "bricks" of a house or building. Without wisdom however, those bricks would never become a house, at least, not a successful one.

Jesus gave us an example of a wise house builder:

Matthew 7:24–25 (New King James Version)
24 "Therefore whoever hears these sayings of Mine, and does them, I will liken him to a wise man who built his house on the rock:
25 and the rain descended, the floods came, and the winds blew and beat on that house; and it did not fall, for it was founded on the rock.

So if we use this example of the "wise man", we learn that knowledge can be used to inform our choices. Wisdom is made up of informed choices and actions. Once we have the "bricks", that knowledge we need, we can then apply those bricks in the correct fashion and build a "house". That's wisdom.

What does it take to build a house?

You need blueprints: a vision

You need enough resources: supplies, money and a budget.

You need a strong foundation: the Rock.

You need helpers: a good team.

You need to know the weather patterns. What kind of elements are going to be coming against your structure? Snow? Rain? Flooding? Hurricanes? Earthquakes?

In the business world you could account for things like:

What kinds of competition will you encounter?

Or what kinds of challenges and obstacles will you encounter?

Are there any unforeseen expenses you did not consider yet?

These are all sample questions — it is not a full list.

<u>Planning in Advance</u>

A wise builder plans for all of this in advance, and builds a team that can withstand and overcome any of those obstacles. This applies to any business, family, church or organization.

So every leader is a kind of "builder". Leaders are builders of many different kinds of things: vision, teams, profits, productivity, company morale, for example. A wise leader builds on a solid rock, and thus will succeed. In the context of the above parable, Jesus is telling us that His Word is the Rock we should build on.

The nemesis: Foolishness

So I said that every leader is a builder. But that does not mean all leaders are wise builders. Some are foolish, unfortunately. They fail to account for some, or all, of the major factors that may come against their business, their employees, their organization, or their team of volunteers.

Jesus continues the above parable with a second builder, a foolish one.

Matthew 7:26–27 (New King James Version)
26 "But everyone who hears these sayings of Mine, and does not do them, will be like a foolish man who built his house on the sand: 27 and the rain descended, the floods came, and the winds blew and beat on that house; and it fell. And great was its fall."

So here we see the foolish builder (foolish leader) has built a house on shifting sands. There is no stability to that. If things are always changing and nothing is solid, or established, a business or organization will suffer. It will not survive.

Leadership collapses with foolish choices and actions.

Is the leader neglecting finance?

What about inventory? Is it sufficient?

Is the leader caring properly for his or her staff or volunteer team?

Did the leader establish a set of acceptable policies and procedures?

Did that leader put the right people into the right positions?

Can the business or organization be reached, discovered, or found by those who may need it?

Some "houses" (aka teams, businesses, churches, families, etc) may crumble slightly. Others may collapse completely. Others are completely successful and stand the test of time.

It all starts with planning in advance and building a wise foundation. We can prevent that kind of failure by starting off wisely and applying knowledge in sound ways.

Start by getting all the facts and applying them properly to your situation. When considering a leadership role, or even a self-employed business, read up on the topic, do your research. Get your blueprint, get your bricks (knowledge), and get help as needed. Don't assume you know everything. Allow others with more experience to speak into your life. Dig down into the topic, and get yourself rooted in your situation before making any major moves.

A Solid Foundation

We should build our teams up. Let's show our people we appreciate them, build up their morale, and their success. But we need a solid foundation underneath our team or else all of that building will collapse under pressure. And foundations take time to establish.

So start on the solid Rock. Follow the words of Jesus. When we do build up our teams and businesses, the pre-planned foundation will be able to support them. That's how wisdom brings success.

Chapter 12 - Respect Vs Disrespect

~

On the very last day of my employment as a grocery department manager for a store, I was thanked by one of our regular sales representatives. He shook my hand and wished me well on my new venture into the world of writing. He made sure to tell me how much he appreciated the way I treated him and other representatives that visited the store.

Sadly, he is used to being disrespected and verbally abused by other managers. But with me, he noted I was always courteous, and polite.

I thanked him back and smiled, telling him that my name, Curtis, actually does mean "courteous". I explained that I have always tried to live up to my name. He smiled back with acknowledgement and wished me well again.

After that encounter, and a few others, it dawned on me that I had made a positive impact in the local retail industry among certain people. I demonstrated the leadership trait known as respectfulness.

Respect is the backbone of leadership. It really does not matter how talented or skilled or knowledgeable a leader is if he or she lacks the basic respect required to lead a team.

<u>What is Respect?</u>

As people, we all need respect in order to thrive. It is built into the very fabric of our humanity, to require respect. But what exactly is respect?

Respect, in its verb form, is the quality of having a high regard or esteem for someone or something. It is the act of valuing someone or something. To give respect is to give importance and dignity.

Respectful leaders esteem their volunteers or employees as valuable. A respectful leader sees their team members as people, not objects or numbers. And not only that, but respectful leaders also ensure they communicate such respect to their team.

A truly respected team will always know that they are respected. That's because respectful leaders make the effort to communicate on a regular basis.

A lot of leaders wish they would receive more respect. Well, I think it starts with the leader first. I believe it should be the one leading the team to be the first to show respect. Respect begets respect.

Then as you, the leader, manager, pastor, or boss, take the initiative to show others that you value them, they will in turn be more likely to reciprocate.

Little things that we do amount to a lot in the eyes of others. For instance, I never realized how far my usual courtesy would go with that sales rep.

Here's another example. Years ago I was in transition between retail positions. After resigning from the old position at the last company, and getting settled into my new position, I had a visitor come to the store.

It was my old boss. She came in to show her appreciation for me and how I had trained my replacement properly. She wanted to ensure that she had said goodbye to me and was not sure that she had done so while I was still at her store. So she wished me well and told me I would always be welcome to return if the opportunity was there. I was shown respect. And it made me feel great.

It's those little details that make a huge impact on our teams. I mean, I was not even working for her anymore, but my old boss took the initiative to find me and express appreciation.

That is impressive. It's a great example of respect.

<u>The Bible teaches us:</u>

1 Peter 2:17 (New King James Version)
17 Honor all people. Love the brotherhood. Fear God. Honor the king.

Here, honour means respect. From the Biblical perspective, I believe God created all people. That means we all have intrinsic worth to Him. We were originally made in His image. That means we are valuable simply for being human.

Yes, people can do bad things. That's sin. The sin nature came by human disobedience to God. So not all actions are respectable.

But people themselves are valuable because God says so in His word.

John 3:16 (New King James Version)
16 For God so loved the world that He gave His only begotten Son, that whoever believes in Him should not perish but have everlasting life.

God values people so much He wishes to save everyone from their sin and eternal punishment. He gives everlasting life to all who believe in Jesus Christ and in His death, burial and resurrection.

Now, if you have some other frame of belief that's fine. I respect you still, even if we may disagree on some things. And that's my point.

Respect is about the fact that you have real human beings working for you and alongside you. Even if people in your team are different from you, they are still deserving of respect as human beings.

My world view helps me to respect my team. Respected teams are far more likely to be effective and productive.

<u>Respect Is More Than A Philosophy</u>
Respect cannot just be a philosophy or talking point. It must be shown, or demonstrated. Thus, respect is a way of behaving, fueled by a Godly worldview.

Here are just a few examples of respectful behaviour from leaders:

-Saying "please" and "thank you" to team members

-Occasionally telling your team you appreciate them.

-Giving team members the benefit of the doubt at times

-Believing the best about your team members, and their efforts.

-Resisting the urge to micro-manage.

-Offering assistance when requested

-Keeping communication lines open and peaceful.

-Not seeing your team as a "threat" to you.

-Doing what is needed to help each team member succeed.

-you don't blow an employee's or volunteer's mistake out of proportion.

-you show empathy and support for employees or team members when they share struggles or concerns with you.

There are so many other things that can be listed here. That's just a sampling of the way we should think and act toward our team.

Respect Builds Trust

As respectful leaders, we will ultimately build trust with our team. Trust is an extremely valuable asset that cannot be synthesized or purchased. It can only be built. Your building tools will include time and respect. There are no shortcuts to genuine trusting relationships. This goes for personal relationships, business relationships, and volunteer organizations.

Being a leader means you are the one who takes the lead. So if you want your people, your employees, or your volunteers, to trust you, you must show them trust first. This is a risk. Some team members may break your trust. In that case, you will know not to trust certain ones. But this does not mean we can ignore trust. No one wants to work in an organization where there is nothing but suspicion, doubt, and accusation. Trust is a must!

In general, a wise leader is able to recognize trustworthy workers, and will invest trust into them. The result can be mutual, growing trust, and good results in the team.

<u>Trust Is A Treasure</u>

Trust is precious. Never take it for granted. Once trust is lost, it is extremely hard to regain. Trust is something we must all earn, regardless of what role we play in a team (leader or follower). So I would even venture to call trust a "treasure". If you are currently leading your team with mutual trust and respect, consider yourself extremely wealthy!

<u>The Evil Nemesis: Disrespect, Narcissism, and Gas-lighting</u>

I am sure most of you have heard the term "Gas-lighting" these days. The term comes from a 1944 thriller-suspense drama called "Gas Light". The movie stars Ingrid Bergman. In it the devious and evil husband intentionally drives his wife mad by making her doubt her perception of reality.

The term has been used a lot in recent years to describe what many people are suffering at the hands of their spouses, family members or coworkers.

In actuality gas-lighting is a form of disrespect.

There are a lot of resources available to help people who are being subjected to gas-lighting, so I won't attempt to cover everything here.

I will give a few examples though. A bad leader is one who gas-lights their team. They will often do things like the following:

-They say something one day, only to deny saying it a week later
-They always place all of the blame on the worker if a project fails (they never own up or take responsibility for their actions)
-They give a specific and unusual set of instructions to the employee, only to reprimand them a few weeks later for following said instructions.
-They demand their worker or department head resolve a problem but refuse to offer any hints or clues as to their desired solution.

Employee then offers a solution, only to get criticized.

-They tend to withhold important information

-They attempt to make their subordinates or team members feel inferior.

-They do odd things, then refuse to admit to it. They want their teams to question their own perception of events.

-They play favourites, and compare other team members to their "pet employee"

-They lack any real empathy for the feelings, concerns, or troubles of the team members

-They may even promote a team member to a position of authority, only to belittle them and bypass them entirely.

-They may have "spies" reporting team members' actions

A disrespectful leader will sometimes resort to these (and many other) methods to gain unhealthy control over their team members. This manipulation is extremely toxic. No trust or success can bloom in such a swampy, stale, and hazardous environment. Good leadership has no manipulation or gas-lighting in it. Those who have no idea how to inspire or respect others will often resort to such nasty tactics.

Narcissist Leaders

Another popular term today is narcissism. This describes anyone who is self-focused, and sees others as only a means to a selfish end. They are manipulators who play mind games and use things like gas-lighting to hide their own insecurities. Narcissists are also bullies. He or she wants to put you down to make himself or herself feel better. Bullies are those who use an imbalance in power to belittle those who have less power than themselves. Again, the root problem is disrespect. Every human being from the lowest rank to the highest is equally valuable in worth. The narcissist leader refuses to admit or consider that fact. Thus they generally lack any empathy toward anyone whom they consider "beneath them".

A leader who fails to recognize the inherent worth of his or her people is more likely to fall into these despicable practices.

There are few things as troubling as a disrespectful leader.

Here are just some of the results from this kind of toxic leadership. Their employees or team members can often feel:

-stress
-fear
-doubt
-anxiety
-lower productivity due to stress levels
-distrust
-self-doubt
-depression
-inability to think or function due to extreme bullying or anxiety
-desire to quit/leave the team
-resentment

A leader is responsible for the overall atmosphere of the workplace or team environment. So if you walk into a place and sense a kind of tension or unease, that is usually a sign of problems.

<u>Beating Disrespect</u>

In order to conquer disrespect, we first need to be aware of it in our own behaviour as leaders. It's easy to point the finger at others. But it requires humility to look at ourselves honestly. Humble honesty is powerful. If at some point you were made aware of something disrespectful you said or did, it needs to be carefully considered. This does not mean we accept that observation blindly. It means we evaluate our own behaviours to see if we have any bad habits that inhibit powerful and effective leadership.

We may accidentally gas-light someone with the wrong choice of words. For instance, let's pretend that I was told by an employee "I need help learning this program", and I turn around and tell them "That should have been easy to learn". Whether I realize it or not, I have just practiced gas-lighting. I just invalidated that employee's need for assistance. It does not matter how easy or hard the program is. It does not matter if everyone else learned it quickly. What matters is that I just made this employee feel worse.

Even if I do help them, they will now feel inferior or insufficient due to my careless comment. This is an example of ineffective leadership.

So rather than say something that invalidates their experience, I should instead reply with a comment like: "Absolutely! How can I help you learn?" This validates their need for assistance and makes them feel included and capable. Once I train them and they start using that program successfully, I can return later and praise their progress. This will bolster their morale and improve performance.

What the narcissist leader is blind to, is that showing respect to their team is what actually strengthens a leader. They wrongly think that tearing others down is the way to build themselves up. This is the mentality of a small-minded, insecure person.

In reality, when a leader chooses to engage in disrespectful behaviour and speech, he or she is ultimately damaging himself or herself. Their manipulation, narcissism, gas-lighting, favouritism, and lack of empathy will drive good workers or volunteers away, and keep productivity stifled.

When we choose to consistently show respect, it will give our team the opportunity to reciprocate. Then the treasure of trust can be formed. You will see your team members rise to new heights. This is what makes leaders and their teams truly powerful and unstoppable.

Conclusion

~

In order to close out this book, I'd like to share a story.

I am thankful to have a hand in influencing, serving, and leading youths and adults as a pastor.

For the last decade, I have been teaching and training up a particular youth in our church, who is now a young adult. I shared my Biblical knowledge and life experiences with him. I was a role model for him. I introduced him to music and taught him the basics of piano. I eventually let him, and others, shadow me on the worship team. I play digital piano and do the lead vocals. He would use my smaller secondary keyboard and accompany me with the other worship team members. He has yet to sing, but I leave that choice up to him.

At the time of this book's publishing, he has full time employment, has his own savings account, and even purchased his own portable digital piano. He uses that piano in church faithfully every week in our Sunday worship services. I never asked him to do that, but he saw that's what I did. Back in 2015 I bought a digital piano, and brought it to church. I am still using it. So he chose to copy that example.

He even became a junior member of our leadership and board team at the church. This to me is what being a leader is all about: raising others up into greatness.

He now follows my example in many ways.

What a delight to see my example copied and enhanced. There is no question that he will go on to become even more skilled on the piano than me.

What is the mark of a good leader? It comes down to positive consistent respect and healthy relationships. You can develop a trusting, successful, cheerful team by practicing the traits described in this book. Introduce them to why you do what you do, and let them see your passion and vision for the work. Treat them like they matter, because they do.

I hope that this book has been helpful to you in your own endeavours as a team leader or pastor or manager. May the Biblical leadership principles brought forth in this book help to bring you and your team success!

Thank you for reading!

Please feel free to leave a written review if you're so inclined. It would be appreciated.

If you would like to connect with me, you can find me at
www.medium.com/@curtisaonthego .